Sharon Calhoun

Truly Said Devotionals – Volume One

Austin Macauley Publishers™
London • Cambridge • New York • Sharjah

All Bible quotes are referenced in the Copyrights Notes page, where applicable.

Ordering Information
Quantity sales: Special discounts are available on quantity purchases by corporations, associations, and others. For details, contact the publisher at the address below.

Publisher's Cataloging-in-Publication data
Calhoun, Sharon
Truly Said Devotionals – Volume One

ISBN 9781643788227 (Paperback)
ISBN 9781645758501 (Hardback)
ISBN 9781645758518 (ePub e-book)

Library of Congress Control Number: 2021925227

www.austinmacauley.com/us

First Published 2022
Austin Macauley Publishers LLC
40 Wall Street, 33rd Floor, Suite 3302
New York, NY 10005
USA

mail-usa@austinmacauley.com
+1 (646) 5125767

It has honored me to have a young man who has articulated my book cover theme in one powerful image. The designer of my book cover is my son, Israele Bonsignore; who is a talented artist/designer and mighty prophet of God. He has had infinite patience with his mother, whose is of a generation of baby boomers, who had to become tech savvy as older adults. It has been a blessing to have Israele as my own in-house IT Professional and Web Designer. I am appreciative and honored to have my son Israele join me in making *Truly Said Devotionals – Volume One* a reality!

Introduction

God, the Holy Spirit, knows each of us intimately. Through this intimate relationship, the Holy Spirit knows the processes we are most receptive to hearing from Him. Over the years, I've received revelations via the use of similes, metaphors, nature, and interactions with others. These experiences dug deeper into what can be seen. They revealed a truth that activated 'a-ha moment', epiphany, or a catharsis, in my once limited understanding.

I have been enlightened via this knowledge and it has produced a deeper perception, clarity, and instruction. In addition, this knowledge has transformed my beliefs/views of myself, others, and my world/environment, for my betterment.

I have labeled these writings as devotionals. They are based on familiar experiences that occurred throughout my day. After each devotional, there will be a profound statement, that I have labeled as 'Truly Said'. This statement will be a revelation that surfaced from my experiences. It is my hope, that you the reader may experience your own "a-ha" moment and receive enrichment to your Christian life. And secondly, that through your intimate relationship with the Holy Spirit; you may identify how He may communicate to you, by the use of persons, places, and things!

I Hate Exercise

I hated to exercise!

So, I read articles to find an activity to make exercise "tolerable." One article suggested I should single out one activity I liked. I actually liked none, but I told myself to give this idea a chance. I walked on treadmills, rode exercise bikes, stepped on steppers, and used a plethora of other exercise equipment. The result? I still hated to exercise. I continued to seek information to help me overcome this "aversion." Then I read an article that suggested I find an exercise, "suited to my personality." Now, this was encouraging!

I'm an introvert; therefore, to join a gym was out of the question. For me, to exercise at home, would be comfortable. In addition, the article advised the reader to get exercise equipment that wasn't complicated. Encouraged, I tried the treadmill again; assuming I would like the thing better because it was in my "home." So, I bought the treadmill and placed it in front of my big television. Yes, this was perfect! I didn't need to put on a gym outfit, my hair could be a mess, and I could do it, but soon as I walked on the treadmill, it became exasperating; *despite the big*

T.V., the interactive video that showed the terrain I walked on, or as I listened to great music on my iPhone.

Again, nothing suited me. Why? I just don't like exercise, period.

So, I went on a sabbatical from exercise. This day, I was in the drugstore and as I walked the aisles; I saw a bottle of a liquid laxative. Now, I won't give away its name, but it's a nasty, thick, dark, smelly bottle of sludge. I had a flashback, concerning Friday nights as a child. On Fridays, my mother would put us in a line and give us this horrible elixir to "clean us out." I was the eldest and therefore the first in line. I felt like I would heave the very moment I saw her pour the liquid into a spoon. I made a terrible face, as the spoon came towards my mouth, and she said, 'You don't have to like it. Just take it; it's good for you.'

Right there in the drugstore, as I looked at multiple bottles of that god-awful sludge, I had my "a-ha" moment. I expected exercise to be enjoyable, exciting, and sexy. I didn't have to like exercise! I had forgot and minimized the benefits of exercising.

I needed to exercise; not because it felt good, looked good, was easy, or even comfortable. I needed to exercise because it was "good for me." This change of attitude gave me the determination to exercise, despite my dislike. Knowing this truth has helped me in other areas of my life. I don't have to like something; I'll just do it because it's good for me!

Truly Said: 'Just take it, it's good for you!'

Scripture: "No discipline is enjoyable while it is happening—it's painful. But afterward, there will be a peaceful harvest of right living for those who are trained in this way." (New Living Version, Hebrews.12.11)[i]

I Want to Learn from My Own Mistakes

I remembered when my son said, "I want to learn from my own mistakes."

Recently, in a conversation, someone remarked, "Bought sense is the best sense." These were the same words, I heard from my son.

As soon as they finished the remark, I heard these words resound in my head, *No, no, no!*

I've learned through many years of trials that this saying isn't true; "bought sense is not the best sense." Oh, how I wished to have avoided painful consequences, by listening to the wise council, instead of learning through experience!

I thought about the wisdom received when I was a young Christian. My mature Christian mentor said, "In my life, I've gone through some hard and painful struggles. I've paid a price for the wisdom and the lessons learned. So, if you'll listen to what I've learned, you won't have to pay that same price."

That wisdom my mentor passed on, became one of my most powerful lessons. It saved me from many heartaches and consequences; by simply listening to the council of other people.

The more I reflected on the significance of these words from this adage, I came to my own conclusion. For me, bought sense will never be the "best sense"; it's just too costly!

Truly Said: It is better to 'borrow' sense than to 'buy' sense.

Scripture: "Plans go wrong for lack of advice: many advisers bring success." (Proverbs.15.22)

Don’t Get Stuck in the Mud

As I browsed online, I saw an article with pictures of a baby elephant wallowing in a pool of mud. In addition, there was an adult elephant that stood by the pool; its trunk stretched towards the chubby baby. The next picture showed that the baby had moved away from the adult. The article explained that the adult was frantic because of the probable danger to the baby. Should the baby continue in the mud, it could become trapped and suffocate.

After reading the article, my spiritual antennas went up! I recalled the times when I stayed in the mud. My mud had been self-pity—me having an emotional tantrum and my refusal to snap out of it. And sometimes my mud was depression or anger at injustice or hurt.

Then I had an epiphany; thrashing about in the mud was a metaphor for my choice to remain trapped in the past. I had ignored the consequences of staying in the unforgiving mire of my spiteful negative feelings. Also, I had to admit to myself that I had choked the word of God by remaining in the mud. But this time, it reminded me of a loving God, who desired to lift me out of the mire, put me on solid ground, help me to release the past, and ultimately renew my hope for tomorrow. No more wallowing in the mud for me!

Truly Said: Wallowing in the mud can 'soil' our Body, Soul, and Spirit!

Scripture: "He lifted me out of the pit of despair, out of the mud and the mire. He set my feet on solid ground and steadied me as I walked along." (Psalm.40.2)

Where Can I Hide?

Living in the desert, I would sit outside in the morning's cool before the scorching sun would force me inside. As I sat in my comfy chair, I caught glimpses of the wildlife stirring. I had to squint to see the birds perched in the trees. The birds' colorings blended into the tree branches and foliage. A rabbit surprised me as he hopped across the road. I didn't see him; the surrounding bushes had hidden him. Then, out of the corner of my eye, I spotted a lizard. The lizard crawled on the stucco walls and his skin of tan and green melded him into the environment.

Originally, I am from Detroit, Michigan. Because of Michigan's changeable weather, I had few occasions to just sit outside and watch the animals in their natural habitat. However, this day in the desert of California, I took notice. I thought, *Wow, Lord, you created these animals to be camouflaged, to disguise them in their surroundings. Lord, why can't I hide in my environment; especially from my enemies?*

Then there was a reply to my reflections, through my thoughts, *I never designed you a Christian to be hidden in your environment or the world. I have called you as a*

Christian to be a witness and to confront the enemy of this world. I didn't make you to live 'undercover.'

This answer came blunt and quick. *My God made everything for a purpose; and this day, I learned that He made me stand out.*

Truly Said: God purposefully didn't give us a camouflage suit!

Scriptures: "The only recommendation we need is you yourselves. Your lives are a letter written in our hearts; everyone can read it and recognize our good work among you." (2 Corinthians.3.2)

"In this same way, let your good deeds shine out for all to see." (Matthew.5.16)

Quote: "Preach the gospel at all times. If necessary, use words." St. Francis of Assisi.

You're Not Done!

All my senses came alive when the waiter set my plate in front of me. My eyes beheld the Rib-Eye steak with just the perfect amount of fat curled around the edges. I inhaled an aroma of char from the sizzling beef. My taste buds drooled for the first taste of a savory morsel. I felt the glide of the steak knife as I cut into the center; then I realized my steak wasn't med-rare. I immediately waved for the waiter. He came to the table, and I informed him, "My steak wasn't medium rare." He apologized and said he would take the steak back to the kitchen to be "re-fired."

Curiously, I asked the young man, when he set my steak before me for a second time, 'What does it mean, to take my steak back to the kitchen to be "re-fired"?'

He responded, "When I tell the chef that a steak has to be 're-fired,' it means that the steak wasn't cooked to the customer's satisfaction."

I gave no further thought to his words; I was ready to devour the steak that had my mouth watering.

However, as I drove home, I reflected upon the words, 're-fire'. I had prepared for retirement and looked forward to a leisurely life (which suited my "languid" personality)! Yet intuitively I knew that my life wouldn't be so relaxed.

Before I retired, I considered becoming a Christian writer, but as retirement came; I put that notion out of mind. After all, I was done working and had no desire to try something new. Then I had a spiritual revelation, from God concerning my personal meaning for "re-fire," I wasn't "done" to God's satisfaction. I may have retired from secular work, but God was directing me to "re-fire" for His Kingdom's work!

Truly Said: God will 're-fire' us until we are done, to his satisfaction.

Scripture: "When Joshua was an old man, the Lord said to him, 'You are growing old, and much land remains to be conquered." (Joshua.13.1)

What's Your Status?

We're all familiar with the phrase, "What's your status?" At work, we have used the phrase to find out the progress of a project. On Facebook, we have used the phrase as a "post," to communicate how we're feeling, what is going on with our lives, and what headway we've made in some area in our lives. "What's your status?" or "what's the status?" means someone wants to know, what's going on, or what's your progress.

My son and I were discussing faith, and he said, "I believe that faith is, not requiring a status update from God."

His revelation was a profound "a-ha" moment for me! How many times have I desired God to give me a brief of what was happening, or the progress towards the manifestation of my prayers? I wanted a "status" update from the Creator of the universe! However, to trust God means I had to believe in His goodness, mercy, wisdom, and sovereignty of His divine nature.

This revelation located me! I needed to accept that God will not reveal what may take place behind the scenes! I had to trust him to work out things for my good. And I can't expect to receive a progress report from him.

Truly Said: God isn't on Facebook; therefore, we need not look for His status.

Scripture: "Trust in the Lord, with all your heart; do not depend on your own understanding." (Proverbs.3.5)

Are You Living a Fairy Tale?

I shook my head as I listened to some of my clients express their rationale for stealing. However, I wasn't surprised; I heard this same rationale from two young men in a store parking lot. My clients and these two young men; believed it was justifiable to steal from a store because the merchants charged "too much" for their goods, or if they didn't like the owner.

Then a thought came to my mind, and I asked my clients, "Are you living a life of fiction or a life of a fairy tale?"

At first, I had to ask myself, where did that thought come from? Then I decided, to go with it came back to my question. I shared that its human nature to desire to live a life of fiction or a fairy tale. I defined a fairy tale as being a sequence of improbable events finishing up with a "happily-ever-after" ending. However, life in a fairy tale isn't reality.

I challenged them to think about the following stories and fairy tales:

Robin Hood:	It justifies you to steal from the rich because you are stealing to give back to the poor. But did you give any of your goods to the less fortunate?
Pied Piper of Hamelin:	It justifies you to retaliate because someone wrongs you; doesn't matter if it harms innocent people.
The Emperor's New Clothes:	You have relationships with people who tell you what you want to hear, and avoid people who will tell you the truth.
Beauty and the Beast:	You choose people who you know are bad for you but believe you can change them.
Little Red Riding Hood:	Someone warned you to stay out of specific neighborhoods but ignored their warning and nearly lost your life.

As I told them the fairy tales, we all laughed. Then I related to them how much these stories rang true to their erroneous beliefs concerning their actions. I finished by saying, that fairy tales can entertain and amuse us, but the end of those stories isn't based on our reality.

After the group was over, I knew I had to personalize our discussion. I can't live my life having erroneous beliefs concerning myself, others, and my world. When I want to see my life as a fairy tale and ignore the truth; it will be the opposite of the happy ending I imagined.

Truly Said: Living a life of self-deception won't end with a happily-ever-after.

Scripture: "Investigate my life, O, God, find out everything about me; Cross-examine and test me, get a clear picture of what I'm about." (The Message Version Psalm.139.23)[ii]

What Is Hindering Your Journey?

In the beginning, most of us can identify with the feelings of excitement as we start the journey of fulfilling a dream. The future benefits of the completion of our dreams gave us the energy to sustain our endeavors. But as time passed, errors and difficulties would diminish our progress and process.

When I had a creative moment, that I would take my blogs and ideas for blogs and compile them into a devotional. I was so enthusiastic. However, as I wrote, I came across several obstacles. My computer was acting up and I'm still deficient in identifying what or how to fix specific features in Windows 10. I rewrote several blogs to include in the devotional, but it appeared I lacked ideas to create new devotions. Then, my body got a "virus," and I didn't have the emotional or physical strength to write or type anything. As I was recuperating, I wondered if writing a devotional wasn't such a good idea. Maybe I was mistaken; perhaps I didn't have the ability or creativity to write anything! Who was I kidding?

Then, during my convalescence as I watched television, I heard a young man say these words to voters, "If your vote wasn't so important, some politicians wouldn't be doing all they could to stop you from voting."

Sometimes when things are tough, I can second guess myself; especially when I desire to do work on something new. In my struggles towards achievement, I sometimes forget that there is an enemy, called Satan. The epiphany for this day; to remember when my plans to do good are thwarted, that it is the nature of Satan to discourage and discredit. It must determine me to persevere because the enemy's tactics are the validation of the importance of my work.

Truly Said: If it wasn't important to God, Satan wouldn't try to stop you!

Scripture: "We don't want Satan to outsmart us. We know how he does his evil work." (New International Reader's Version, 2 Corinthians.2.11)[iii]

You Can't Find Your Love in a Hospital

In a Co-Ed Residential Treatment Group, I tried to communicate the negative consequences of clients seeking to have sexual contact/intimate relationships. I used therapeutic interventions and intellectual reasonings, but they continued to look at me as if I spoke in a foreign language.

Then one client yelled out, "Just tell them, two sickies don't make a wellie."

"They're right. Looking for someone in here is like going to the hospital to look for amate," quipped another client in response!

All the clients laughed, and so did I. I had never heard that expression before, but it made perfect sense.

After group, I thought of specific times when I wasn't emotionally ready or in the right frame of mind to begin a relationship with the opposite sex. At those times, I began relationships with men just as unhealthy as I. These negative relationships were stressful, frustrating, conflictual, and just downright unproductive. When those relationships ended my emotional being was further damaged.

I had to remember that when I am sick, physically, emotionally, or spiritually, I lack the clarity to make healthy choices. Only, when I'm "well," can I make positive decisions in life. And I will make a choice to heal or recover, before I start another relationship.

Truly Said: When I am a 'sickie,' I lack the ability to find a 'wellie'.

Scripture: "Don't be fooled by those who say such things, for 'bad company corrupts good character." (New Living Translation Version, 1 Corinthians 15:33)

What Would Your Mother Say?

I have heard people make the excuse; "So and so did it too." Lately, I have heard politicians use this excuse to rationalize their behaviors. And, I have heard this excuse on many occasions from my children, my clients, and other people. They all used this excuse to defend their actions.

One day, when I heard this particular excuse, I thought to myself, *Would this person give this excuse to their mothers?* At first, I believed this question to be amusing, but in truth, it wasn't.

I recalled, as most of us, can recall, when we made this excuse, "everybody is doing it," to our mothers.

I remembered my mother's response vividly, "If so and so jumped off a bridge, would you do it too?" Then the next words from my mother were, "I don't care what so and so is doing; all I know is you better not do it."

Our earthly parents wouldn't accept this particular excuse for my wrongful behaviors, and neither will our heavenly Father. The characteristics of a mature Christian are; accepting responsibility for **"our"** actions, confessing **"our"** sins, and bringing fruits of repentance. I can't live my life playing the blame game; my mother wouldn't allow it!

Truly Said: When we stand before God at Judgment Day, He will not accept the excuse of 'So and so did it too!

Scripture: "And even if it be true that I have erred, my error remains with myself." (English Standard Version, Job.19.4)[iv]

We All Are Human

My son was going through some stressful experiences. One day when I called him, he was curt and snappy. His words didn't upset or hurt me. I knew he was having some challenges and after we ended the call, I prayed for him.

The next day he called and apologized, with these words, "Ma, please forgive how I spoke to you yesterday. I just wasn't my best self."

I told him, I understood and prayed for him. We chatted more and when the call ended; I reflected over his words. "He wasn't his best self." The impact of these words amazed me and how I viewed myself and others. I considered how many times I wasn't my best self, and how I wished for the people to be more understanding. I thought of the times when people were blunt or snippy towards me. Upon reflection, I wished to have been more sympathetic and understanding. I knew they were good people. It just happened that this particular day; they weren't their "best self."

There will be occasions when people in our lives, may not be themselves; for whatever reason. I choose to remember we're all human and have bad days. As a Christian, I must discern when people are having a difficult time and not personalize their words or actions towards us. I must be ready to pray for them and realize that I will also have bad days.

Truly Said: We all will have days when we're not our 'best self!

Scripture: "Most of all, love one another deeply. Love erases many sins by forgiving them." (New International Reader's Version, 1 Peter.4.8)

Correction to Stop Destruction

Sometimes, in prayer, I have had to stop and ask God; how do I pray? This particular time, it concerned me for a young person. This young adult continued to engage in criminal behaviors and associate with dangerous relationships. I had prayed that they would "see the light" and end their behaviors. But it appeared my petitions weren't working, and I was afraid their young life would become a casualty.

Then I remembered a portion of scripture; our prayers aren't answered because we're praying amiss. So, I asked the Holy Spirit to reveal the words to pray and the answer immediately appeared, "Pray for the correction to stop the destruction."

These words were an "a-ha" moment for me; simply presented, but powerful. When we pray for someone, we certainly don't wish for them to receive the painful consequences of their sinful actions. However, sometimes it is the repercussions of our actions that are the motivators to change.

As I meditated on my instructions on how to pray, I realized that God's correction doesn't destroy a person, but the correction of the world, surely will. I was being instructed to "pray God's correction to stop the destruction" and to believe God knew how to administer His correction.

So, I prayed according to the words God gave me; for the "correction to stop the destruction." Shortly the police arrested this young person. Their arrest was God's correction; the young person's criminal behaviors in the streets could have easily taken their life. I learned to pray this prayer for others; for God to send the correction to stop the destruction. Our Father God knows the form, manner, and timing of the correction we all need.

Truly Said: God's correction can spare our lives; the world's correction will take our lives.

Scripture: "For the Lord corrects those he loves, just as a father corrects a child in whom he delights." (New Living Translation Version, Proverbs 3:12)

I Allowed It

A person asked me, "How could you forgive him; especially with all the malicious things he did to you?"

As a Christian, the natural answer would be, "Because the Bible commands us to forgive your brother." However, to forgive your brother is an easy answer. The difficult answer; I had to forgive myself. This revelation has been liberating, yet painful.

I reflected on my journey towards self-acceptance and to conquer my own unhealthy behaviors. As a psychotherapist, I've been cognizant of my people's pleasing and co-dependent behaviors. Too many times, I had placed others' needs before my own. Too many times, I had allowed people to take advantage of me, disrespect me, and emotionally abuse me. I took part in these unhealthy behaviors because I erroneously believed I could make people accept and like me.

Yes, people abused me, however, I allowed them to abuse me. I had to forgive the people for hurting me, more importantly, I had to forgive myself. I had to forgive myself for my willingness to accept abuse to secure the acceptance and good-will of others.

I knew, as a therapist, erroneous beliefs about myself could keep me in bondage to others. I had to overcome my negative beliefs of unworthiness, low self-esteem, and self-hatred. I had to free myself from needing the validations of others at any cost. I had to find myself in the scriptures which said, I was accepted in the Beloved and made in the image of God. I had to remind myself I didn't have to work to be accepted by God and therefore why should I work to be accepted by others?

It has been easy to forgive them than to forgive myself. However, this is what I've learned; to forgive myself for not stopping their abuse towards me—before it started.

Truly Said: Stop abuse; know who you are and whose you are!

Scripture: "I will give up whole nations to save your life, because you are precious to me, and because I love you and give you honor." (Good News Translation Version, Isaiah.43.4)[v]

You Must Take the Whole Banana!

We all have experienced envy or jealousy; it is part of our human nature. However, envious and jealous feelings can deceive us. These so-called "green-eyed monster" emotions can embody the entire picture of what someone owns or how someone looks. These feelings deceive us into only looking at the attractive attributes of those we may envy.

I was praying and confessing to the Lord the feelings of jealousy I had experienced towards someone.

As I asked for forgiveness, an "a-ha" instruction came from the Holy Spirit, "Take the whole banana."

Shocked, I wondered if I had heard correctly.

Then I had these thoughts that clarified what I had heard, *Do you desire just the beautiful parts of their world? Or are you prepared to take the whole banana; the good, the bad, and the ugly of their lives?*

I had to stop my prayers and consider the instructions. I was divorced, and I had envied a woman's married life. I thought about the entire life of the woman I envied and asked myself, *Did I want her entire married life?* I recalled the times that this specific woman lamented regarding her husband's emotional abuse, his controlling actions, and condescending comments towards her. I remembered situations where I had heard her husband's negative remarks towards his wife. *Did I want to live with a man like that?*

I thought about how I envied a couple who had just purchased a home but later remembered they shared how they were "house-poor" and struggling to make ends meet. *Did I want that part of their lives?*

Oh, and I remembered, that on my job, the envy I felt towards a person who received a promotion. I heard this person express the frustration she had experienced because her boss took credit for their ideas, made them the "fall guy" for all the departments' troubles, and criticized this person in the presence of others. *Did I want to deal with that aspect of her promotion?*

As I reflected on these three situations, I had to admit; I was unwilling to have to take everything that encompassed their marriage, home, and promotion. I was honest with myself; I didn't want to "take the whole banana."

These words revelatory words taught me an intervention to manage my envious feelings. I had to remember that all of us have the good, the bad, and the ugly in our lives. If I desired and coveted the life of someone else; I had to "take the whole banana!"

Truly Said: You can't just take a 'piece' of someone's life!

Scripture: "Do not long for anything that belongs to your neighbor. Do not long for your neighbor's house, wife, male or female servant's ox or donkey." (New International Reader's Version, Exodus.20.17)

Serenade in the Courtroom

I interviewed a new client. She spoke of her gratitude for the judge mandating her to substance abuse treatment instead of jail time. As we continued our conversation, she unashamedly offered the circumstances that led the judge to make his ruling.

The client said she had appeared before the judge's bench for the third time. His Honor reviewed her case. He reminded her of the many times, he exercised leniency towards her drug-related charges. In addition, the judge read the many times that he mandated treatment instead of jail time. His Honor reminded the client, despite given leniency, how she continued to violate probation.

This time, everyone in the courtroom speculated that it would sentence her to jail time. Before the judge announced his decision, he asked her to give him one good reason she shouldn't be sent to jail. I suppose everyone thought, including the judge; she wouldn't have a credible answer.

Then the client looked straight at the judge, opened her mouth, and sang! She sang the song, *Everything Must Change,* composed by Benard Ighner. This particular song was a standard in the '70s and performed by many well-known artists.

These were the words she sang from the first verse of the song:

Everything must change, nothing stays the same.
Everyone must change nothing stays the same.

It stunned the judge and everyone in the courtroom. First of all, she could actually sing. Then, she seriously defended herself in the song without a drop of shame. It shocked the entire courtroom!

His Honor shook his head and remarked, "I had no one serenade me in my courtroom."

The judge said it convinced him this time; she understood and believed the words of the song. Satisfied with her sincerity, he gave her the absolute last chance; residential substance abuse treatment instead of jail.

As I listened to her story, I thought of the times, I made adamant declarations of change. Sometimes the people involved would tire of my use of the same proclamations. Then their belief in my sincerity would wane. Yet I needed to mirror the actions of this young woman. There will be times when I must step out of our comfort zone and do whatever it takes to show my determination to change; to God and to man.

Truly Said: "Everything and everyone **must** change."

Scripture: "Prove by the way you live that you have repented of your sins and turned to God." (Matthew.3.8)

Ouch! But It Hurts for Good!

I've never been so fascinated with nature. Spending time outside and observing nature, was a benefit of moving to California. I learned many spiritual lessons, just sitting outside.

For about a year, I've sat on my patio and looked at a tree in the next yard. This was a mature tree; however, leaves attached sparsely on its branches. This day, two men were in that yard and they discussed how to cut the tree down.

One man gestured, with his hands in a chopping motion, and said, "We'll cut it here, whoosh. Then cut it here and there; whoosh, whoosh."

From what I heard; they would soon cut the tree down.

A few days afterward, I looked at an arborist hook himself up with his safety lines and cut small branches from the top to the bottom. I surmised that soon the tree would come down. Honestly, I grew worried about how the tree would collapse; the tree towered way above the roof of my home. Would the tree fall on my home?

Weeks passed, and no one showed up to cut the tree down. Then, I watched how the branches grew new leaves.

After a few months, the foliage of the tree budded from its branches. It amazed me to observe its growth daily.

Again, I learned a spiritual lesson from nature; just watching the tree come to life. I've heard the saying, "We all need to be pruned," but I watched the necessity of cutting away old branches. Only when we cut away the lifeless branches of our lives, can we create room for the new branches that will bear living fruit.

Truly Said: Pruning areas of our lives, may hurt; but they are necessary and for our good.

Scripture: "He cuts off every branch of mine that doesn't produce fruit, and he prunes the branches that do bear fruit, so they will produce even more." (John.15.2)

Thankful and Grateful

In my morning devotions, I asked God for a consistent attitude of being thankful. A thought occurred to mind as I prayed, *Remember to be thankful, but don't overlook being grateful.* After I said, "amen" to my prayers, I pondered, *Wasn't thankful and grateful for the same thing?*

As I sat quietly, the Holy Spirit revealed the difference between being thankful and grateful. Sometimes, we just say "thanks" because it's the demonstrative and recognized response to a person's gift or service. Simply, our thanks can be a perfunctory acknowledgment. However, we don't respond to the sacrifice that went into the gesture of giving. *Did we acknowledge the sacrifice or inconvenience that the giver experienced?* The recognition of a person's sacrifice or inconvenience with the gift is the definition of gratitude.

I thought of the last time, someone provided a service for me. I only expressed my thanks for the ride to my appointment. In the future, I would thank them for the ride and express my gratitude. I won't minimize their kindness by just saying "thanks." I will recognize the inconvenience, sacrifice, and willingness to assist me by verbally expressing my gratitude.

Truly Said: Thankful is for the gift or service; grateful is for the sacrifice!

Scripture: "One of then, when he saw that he was healed, came back to Jesu, shouting 'Praise God.' He fell to the ground at Jesus' feet, thanking him for what he had done. This man was a Samaritan." (Luke.17.15-16)

Who Stole Baby Jesus?

It was two weeks before Christmas. I was the supervisor for a residential program and the clients were setting up the holiday decorations. We had a Nativity scene, with statues about four feet tall and they placed them in the front lobby. One client had a family member bring straw for the manger where baby Jesus would lay. We finished decorating the building, and the clients displayed the holiday spirit.

The next day, I came into work and was met at the door by some clients. It upset the clients; someone had taken baby Jesus! They escorted me over to the Nativity scene and baby Jesus wasn't in the manger. I shook my head. My morning began with investigating who took baby Jesus. I went to another wing in the building and saw that someone had baby Jesus in their office.

I asked them, with great annoyance, "Why did you take baby Jesus out of the manger?"

"It is a tradition, you don't place baby Jesus in the manger until Christmas Eve," they answered with confidence.

This early in the day, I didn't have the inclination to reverse their decision. I was glad to find baby Jesus! I simply went back to. the front where the clients were standing. As they stood in front of the nativity scene, I told them that "we" planned to adhere to the tradition of placing baby Jesus in the manger on Christmas Eve. It satisfied the clients, and it relieved me that the mystery was over.

As I went on with my day, every time I would pass the nativity scene, my eyes would fixate on the empty manager. At the end of my day, I stood in front of the manger and a thought came to mind, *Jesus is no longer in the manger.*

I got in my car and as I drove home, the Holy Spirit continued to open my thoughts, *Jesus isn't in the manger, Jesus isn't in the tomb and Jesus isn't on the cross.*

This reality challenged me to remember this Christmas; Jesus isn't the lowly babe in the manger. Jesus has risen and is seated in Heaven with all power and authority.

Truly Said: We celebrate that Jesus has risen on Easter; Jesus has also risen on Christmas!

Scripture: "Then the angel spoke to the woman, 'Don't be afraid!' he said. I know you are looking for Jesus, who was crucified. He isn't here! He is risen from the dead, just as he said would happen. Come, see where his body was lying." (English Standard Version, Matthew. 28.5)

Get a Theme Song!

On my job, I sat in the front office, when the song came on. I looked up at the secretary and smiled. I knew she would get out of her chair to sing, gesture, and sway to the music. The song was *I will survive* by Gloria Gayner. The first time I witnessed the secretary's response to the song; she explained her reactions. She told me how this song got her through a painful divorce. She said whenever she felt sad, mad, or questioned her decision to divorce; she would play this song. Some words of the song were:

At first, I was afraid, I was petrified. Kept thinking I could never live without you by my side. But then I spend so many nights thinking how you did me wrong, and I grew strong, and I learned how to get along.

Oh no, not I, I will survive. Oh, as long as I know how to love, I know I'll stay alive.

The melody and words of the song; gave her the strength to move forward with her life.

As I walked back to my office, I thought how this song had become the secretary's "theme song." Then, I said to myself, *I need a "theme song."* As a Christian, I needed to identify specific songs I could sing that would strengthen me, encourage me, and soothe me. When I got home, I got out the ol' Baptist Hymnal. Even though I'm not a Baptist, I purchased this hymnal because I loved the old songs. I identified specific songs, that I would purpose to sing when I went through a life challenge.

Sometimes, in times of stress, I had to force myself to sing the words of these songs. The words of one song were, *I will bless the Lord at all times.* This particular song, I had to grit my teeth and sing it out. However, I can truthfully say, that singing this song taught obedience to the Lord; despite how I felt.

So, I have specific songs that are, for lack of a better description, my "theme songs." When I can't or don't want to pray, I have purposed to sing these songs. Sometimes with enthusiasm, sometimes with defiance, and sometimes in tears, I will sing these songs to free my soul!

Truly Said: You can't sing, dance and be sad or mad, at the same time!

Scripture: "I will extol the Lord at all times; His praise will always be on my lips." (New International Version, Psalm. 34.1)[vi]

I Was Afraid of Myrtle

I was afraid of Myrtle; Myrtle was my mother. It was a reverential fear. I was mindful of how hard she struggled to keep our family fed, clothed, and sheltered; despite my father's use of alcohol and his gambling. Therefore, I didn't want to disappoint her or make matters more difficult for her by being disobedient.

However, being a teenager, I often had to be punished because I ignored the rules. My mother's punishments were legendary. When I was grounded and couldn't leave the house for any reason except to go to school; I couldn't answer the door or the telephone! Sometimes, when I was punished, I was angry and defiant. However, then sometimes I was sad because I disappointed her.

Back in my day, I wasn't the only teenager that feared their parents. As teenagers, we would often say that we couldn't do something because our parents would "kill us." Yet, there were times I so thankful to use my fear of Myrtle, as an excuse to keep me from doing something I didn't want to do.

On occasions, as a teenager, they offered me drugs or alcohol. I didn't want to try getting high, but I didn't want to be seen as a "goody-two-shoes."

So, I would say, "No, I'm not doing that because if Myrtle found out, she would kill me."

My mother is deceased, and I often think about how she worked so hard to raise us. I believe my fear of her helped me to have a reverential fear of the Lord. I realized that the fear of Myrtle kept me out of some dangerous situations, as a teenager and the fear of the Lord has kept me out of some dangerous situations, as an adult.

Truly Said: "Reverence for your parents, leads to a reverence for God."

Scripture: "The fear of the Lord is a fountain of life, turning a person from the snares of death." (Proverbs.14.27)

Words Can Wait

A friend expressed her desire to confront our co-worker's behavior. As I listened, I believed my friend should wait to address the behavior. The co-worker's rude remarks called for a need for them to have a conversation. However, I reminded my friend, that our co-worker had been undergoing some difficult experiences at home. I suggested to my friend perhaps it wasn't a good time for them to talk. I asked my friend to defer the discussion, for a few days. My friend became upset with my suggestion and despite my advice; had the conversation.

I went back to my office and sat down. I was disturbed because the situation developed into a disagreement between my friend and me. Then, I had a thought, *Words don't spoil.*

Words aren't the same as a cut of meat. Raw meat will spoil if it's not refrigerated. Words aren't the same as meat; words don't spoil if they aren't expressed immediately. I thought about the times, I had said words, that I wished to have waited to say. I thought about the times, I should have taken time to pray and think over the words I wanted to speak.

After this “nugget of wisdom,” I want to remember, to pray, and reflect before I speak, especially when I am hurt or angry. Then perhaps, I will wait before I speak, or not speak at all.

Truly Said: “Words won’t spoil; we can wait to say them!”

Scripture: “Words spoken at the right time are like gold apples in a silver setting.” (Common English Bible w/Apocrypha, Proverbs.25:11)

You Just Don't Know

Tears came to my eyes, as I read about a dear friend, celebrating one year of being free from breast cancer. I remembered how I cried when she posted on Facebook, a video of shaving her hair to donate. As weeks passed, I enjoyed reading about her returning to her private practice as a psychotherapist and talented occupational therapist. I was excited to look at pictures of her hair growing. I was so proud to watch the video of her delivering a speech in the prison, to inform the inmates about breast cancer. I was so blessed to see the posted pictures of her smiling face.

Then, she sent me a private message; she was going through a divorce. It shocked me. From her statuses and pictures posted, one would never know of her pain and sorrow.

As I read the message, I recalled what my mother used to say, "Heap see, but few know."

"I reflected on this wise adage from my mother. It reminded me of the times, I experienced heartbreaking circumstances. All that anyone could see was my smiling face; heap see, but few know." People around me, hadn't any idea of the fight it took, to press on.

Just because a person is smiling, I can't conclude that all is well. They may go through a distressing situation. Reading my friend's message, I thought how important it is to demonstrate kindness to other people; simply because, I just don't know.

Truly Said: Heap see, but few know!

Scripture: "But the fruit of the Spirit is love, joy, peace, patience, "kindness," goodness, faithfulness, gentleness, self-control, against such things there is not law." (God's Word Translation Version, Galatians 5.22) [vii]

What Was My Sin?

I have a prayer pattern to start my devotions. However, I give the Holy Spirit free reign, to change the pattern. My prayer pattern is I enter into His gates with thanksgiving and praise, I ask forgiveness for my sins, pray for the peace of Jerusalem, pray for our country and leaders, pray for missionaries, and then my petitions for myself and others. This particular morning, the Holy Spirit stopped me at "asking forgiveness for my sins."

My thought was, *Did you just pray for the sins you were doing? What about the sins of not doing?*

I had to stop and mull over these words for a minute. Then, I got an "a-ha." The Holy Spirit was reminding me about the need to ask forgiveness for sins of omission. It was easy for me to confess the sins I committed, but I minimized and forgot about the sins of "not" doing something I knew to do.

I reflected on some hurts. My recent hurt came from someone who agreed to help me in a distressful situation and simply didn't show up or call. This person and the experience deeply hurt me. It wasn't what this person did, it was what they didn't do. I remembered the times I reasoned I was too busy to help, too poor to give, didn't want to inconvenience myself and other instances. I had my own sins of omission!

So, I went back to my prayers. I asked the Holy Spirit to reveal my sins of omission; when I knew what to do but didn't.

Truly Said: Sins of commission or omission are equal in the sight of God!

Scripture: "It is a sin when someone knows the right thing to do and doesn't do it." (Common English Version, James.4.7)

Truth Is Truth

A friend came into my office and told me about an encounter. He was entering a party store and there was a young man, leaning against the wall. The young man was dirty, unshaven, and had tracks on his arm; it was obvious he was a drug addict. He asked for some change. My friend told him, he would give him some change, when he came out. My friend bought himself a pack of cigarettes and lit one, as some as he went out the door. Then he turned to the young man, put his hand in his pocket, and pulled out a dollar bill.

The young man turned to him and said, quite seriously, "You need to quit smoking, They're no good for your lungs."

It stunned my friend; he stopped and glared at the young man. He said, "He took another drag on his cigarette, kept his head in his pocket, and thought, *Who does he think he is, telling me to stop smoking because it's bad for me? Here he is all cracked out on drugs, leaning on the wall, begging for change and he has the nerve to chide me about my cigarettes?"*

Then he calmed down and had another thought, *What he said to me is true, despite who he may be.*

"You're right. These cigarettes aren't good for my health," my friend said, as he pulled the dollar out of his pocket, and gave it to the young man.

We didn't have time to finish our conversation as someone came into my office and my friend left out.

When I was alone, I recalled something my son told me. My son said, his father would often tell him, "Hypocrisy doesn't negate the truth." I reflected on these words and the conversation I had with my friend. My friend realized, from his encounter with the young man, truth is truth; no matter who says it.

Truly Said: Hypocrisy doesn't negate the truth.

Scripture: "Jesus said to the people who believed in him, 'You are truly my disciples if you remain faithful to my teachings. And you will know the truth, and the truth will set you free." (New Living Translation, John.8.31-32)

Why Can't I Have Ten Perfect Fingernails?

I was removing polish from my nails and then one nail broke. I shook my head in frustration as I cut and evenly filed my nails.

Then I had a thought, *Why can't I have ten perfect fingernails?*

The response was in another thought, *Your fingernails are like your Christian walk; your Christian walk will never be perfect.*

This scenario happened when I was a new Christian. I was on my Christian "honey-moon" and so in love with Jesus. However, as the months passed, I became so frustrated with being a Christian. I was striving to do everything just right. If I fell short, so committed some sin; I would become discouraged and depressed. I wanted to be a perfect Christian.

This metaphor that came to me, comparing my fingernails to my Christian walk, caused me to remember when I asked Christ to come into my life. The knowledge of Christ accepting me, just as I was a sinner; motivated me to accept Jesus as Savior and Lord. It was on this day a deeper revelation of His Grace, overcame my erroneous beliefs of being a perfect Christian. I was so relieved to know; I didn't have to be perfect.

Truly Said: Salvation is immediate; changing into the image of Christ, is a process.

Scripture: "Or do you despise the riches of His goodness, forbearance, and long-suffering, not knowing that the goodness of God leads you to repentance?" (New King James Version, Romans 2.4)[viii]

What Type of Relationship Is It?

I loved my friend, but there were times our relationship was frustrating. We had good times when we were engaged in activities, such as a movie, concert, or shopping. However, it was at dinner, that I just felt as if, I was only there to listen. If the conversation shifted from talking about her to talking about me, she refocused on herself. For example, we went out to dinner, when I recently completed my divorce. As I talked about my divorce, the conversation switched to her talking about her divorce; five years ago.

I had known my friend for many years before I became a therapist. Now working as, a therapist, I learned I needed to reevaluate our relationship. As a therapist, I listened to clients all day. I didn't expect to have conversations focusing on my needs and personal life. It was necessary for me, to have relationships, where I could have my needs met; to be heard. I had to rethink our relationship. But, when you've known someone for years, it's difficult to break off the relationship; simply because you're moved to a new "place" in life.

I was at home and had the television on; simply for company. I heard a minister speaking and really wasn't listening until I heard the words, "some friendships are just ministry."

The minister explained, "Whether you're a pastor or a minister, or not, some personal relationships are ministry. You can't expect them to meet your needs. You accept that you will be the giver and they would be the receiver; the roles will never change."

I never considered my personal relationships in this manner; it was an epiphany. My friend wasn't a bad person; she just needed a lot of attention. Yet, I needed to change the dynamics of our relationship. I needed to have a friend where sharing our lives would be reciprocal. I accepted the reality; that my friend couldn't give what I needed.

At first, I was sad, that I decreased the time I spent with my friend, but later I had a revelation. When we were together, I would listen to her talk about herself; period. At the time we were together, she was my ministry, and I would accept that role.

Truly Said: Accept the reality, some friends may require more than just a friendship; that friend might simply be your ministry.

Scripture: "Therefore, accept each another just as Christ has accepted you so that God will be given the glory." (New Living Translation Version, Romans.15.7)

Finding God in the Ordinary

Myself, my son, and my sister were having a conversation about faith in God. My son expressed the struggle with keeping the faith while waiting for an answer to prayer. With sharing a birthday, my son and my sister had a special spiritual closeness. His aunt became silent during our discussion, turned to my son, and said, "God wants you to find the miraculous in the mundane."

All was quiet, for a few minutes. We encountered a tangible awareness of the Holy Spirit. Then we discussed, what is the meaning of mundane, in this particular thought? We agreed with this general opinion, regarding this revelation; to seek God in our ordinary daily experiences.

When I was alone, I meditated further on the personal significance of these words to myself. I recalled the times I received uncommon favor. I mentally listed some examples; the bank canceling my overdraft fees, my insurance paying for medication not on the formulary, having no furniture, and finding an apartment fully furnished, and I could go on. These were natural, highly improbable, and extraordinary events; but nonetheless, divinely orchestrated.

After my time of meditation, I purposed daily to see God working in the commonplace and routine situations in my life. Finding God in the ordinary starts with acknowledging his uncommon favor every day.

Truly Said: We will find the miraculous in the mundane.

Scripture: "For the Lord God is a sun and shield; the Lord bestows favor and honor; no good thing does he withhold from those whose walk is blameless." (New International Version, Psalm. 84.11)

The Dragon Couldn't Get In!

I seldom remember my dreams, but this dream caused my spiritual antennas to quickly rise. In this dream, I saw a house with thick, billowing smoke rising from the chimney. Hovering above the smoke, was a dragon. This monster didn't seem to make any attempt to enter the chimney; it faced the chimney and just lingered above the smoke.

When I awoke, it unnerved me from the vivid scene of my dream. *What did it mean?* After fixing a cup of coffee, I sat in the chair and pondered over the dream. Initially, my interpretation of the dream was negative. Perhaps the Holy Spirit was giving me the warning to examine my life and identify any sinful behaviors that warranted repentance.

Then I had an epiphany, when a portion of scripture came to mind, about the aromas from the prayers of the saints. The incense burning from my prayers were rising and floating up the chimney. The dragon was symbolic of evil desiring to enter my home, however, the fragrance of my prayers, prevented his entrance.

Sometimes, when I pray, I wonder if my prayers are being effective? This dream was the Holy Spirit encouraging me concerning the effectiveness of my prayers. I smiled and gave thanks to the Holy Spirit for this message.

Truly Said: Our prayers are a sweet odor to God, but a stench to Satan!

Scripture: “And when he had taken it, the four living creatures and the 24 elders fell down before the lamb. Each one had a harp, and they were holding golden bowls of incense, which are the prayers of God’s people.” (Revelation. 5.8)

What Does God's Voice Sound Like?

When I worked for the Salvation Army Residential Substance Abuse Facility, I would give a motivational talk, using spiritual principles, each morning. I called this talk "Morning Focus", and I would give the client population words of encouragement to reflect upon. This morning, after my talk, a client approached me with a question.

"So, what does God's voice sound like?" he asked innocently.

"What does God's voice sound like?" I repeated his question because I wasn't sure what he meant.

He smirked and answered with skepticism, "Well, you Christians always say that you heard from God. You just said you heard from God; when you were talking."

"So, you're thinking, when Christians say they have heard from God, they are talking about an audible voice?" It stupefied me.

"That's right, and that's why I believe none of you; talking about what God said to you," he spoke with annoyance.

I felt so sorry for him and tears came to my eyes. I did not understand that anyone would come to that conclusion.

I asked him to come to my office; to clarify what I meant, by God speaking to me. I articulated, how Christians are using, our thoughts as a metaphor for God's voice. I gave the example of him being in a session and having an epiphany in the therapeutic discussion. I gave him examples from Jesus's parables and how God uses examples from nature, our environment, and others to speak to us.

He listened and responded quite frankly, "I understand everything you said and it makes sense. But you Christians need to explain what you mean when you are saying to us that God spoke to you. We're just learning about Jesus and being a Christian and you guys need to make things plain."

When he left, we hugged. This client opened my eyes. I reflected on our discussion and purposed in my heart to use my words carefully when speaking to nonbelievers, or new Christians. The purpose of the morning focus wasn't just to encourage clients on the road to recovery, it was to win souls!

Truly Said: God's voice can be found in experiencing people, places, and things.

Scripture: "The fruit of the righteous person is a tree of life, and a winner of souls is wise." (God's Word Translation Version, Proverbs. 11.30)

It Will Work for My Good!

I had mapped out my professional journey after I graduated with my masters' degree in clinical social work. During my volunteer time with an agency for HIV-positive women, I was acquainted with the director of social services, at the Detroit Rescue Mission. The director informed me that the rescue mission would be in a joint venture with a hospital. This venture would be an inpatient program for mentally ill and drug-addicted adults. I was pleased to have the director offer me a position with this new program, but he informed me that the program wouldn't begin for the next six months; and would I still be interested? I was glad to wait until the program began. It would form this program with Christian principles and was what I had hoped for after graduation.

I didn't seek employment for six months because I was waiting for the rescue mission job. After, about five months, the director asked me to come into his office. He informed me that the hospital would continue to open the new program but had canceled the joint venture with the rescue mission. He was very apologetic because he didn't have another position for me.

I left his office, in a panic. I had to rush and find me a job. I was fortunate to get a job with a Mental Health

Agency. I had been working there, for approximately six months, when I met a nurse. This nurse was a new employee at the agency and informed me that she had been working at the hospitals' new program for mentally ill and addicted adults (the same program I was to be used by the rescue mission). She told me that the program had been open for only six months when the hospital closed the program.

I had an epiphany after our conversation. If I had been working with the rescue mission/hospital, I now would be unemployed. Sometimes, I want my journey to be straight and sure and I would become frustrated if I had to make twists and turns. However, despite the detour I had to make with my journey; God turned my disappointment and a negative situation, into one that worked for my good!

Truly Said: Sometimes our journey isn't a straight line from point A to point B.

Scripture: "And we know that for those who love God all things work together for good, for those who are called according to his purpose."

(English Standard Version, Rev.5.8)

Why We Take Medication

As a therapist, I've heard many individuals make this remark, "I will not take any medication because I believe God to heal me."

Early in my profession, I didn't have a response. However, at this particular time, when someone made this remark; a thought entered my mind, *Occupy until He comes.*

I went to my bible and read the scripture that spoke about working until He comes. The Holy Spirit imparted this reasoning, "People need to take medication, so they can continue to work for the kingdom, until they're healed or until I return."

My new response to these precious people of God was to enlighten them on the benefits of the medication. I reminded them of this reality; no one knows when we will be healed. Nevertheless, God expects us to continue to use our gifts and talents to preach the gospel. The role of medication and other interventions; is to assist us to become emotionally and physically whole. We're expected to be fit to work in the kingdom until God manifests our healings.

Truly Said: God never expects us to be out of commission.

Scripture: "And he called his ten servants, and delivered them ten pounds, and said unto them occupy till I come." (King James Version, Luke. 19.13)

Everything Isn't Good for You

I had resolved to get a divorce. It was the best decision for me because my husband was unwilling to commit to marriage. However, despite choosing to divorce; I had to be truthful with myself. I still loved my husband. The truth of my feelings put me on an emotional rollercoaster. One day I hated him; another day I loved him.

I prayed and cried out to the Holy Spirit to help me deal with my feelings. It just seemed my decision to divorce, despite loving him, was such an oxymoron. After I finished my prayer, I had this thought, *Everything you love isn't good for you.* This catharsis was so compelling it took my breath away!

With this release, I could put my feelings for him into a healthy perspective. Sure, I still loved him, but he wasn't good for my spiritual or emotional health. I thought about other things and people I cared for in the past and how I had to withdraw myself from them for my good. I was ready to see I separated myself from these things and people because the love wasn't mutual.

This revelation was the motivation for me to do what was best for me; continue with the divorce. I realized that my sympathies for him were not love; my feelings were grief and regret.

As time went on, I could love my ex-husband as a brother in Christ, because that kind of love didn't require him to reciprocate.

Truly Said: True love requires that we desire the highest good for another person.

Scripture: "Someone will say, 'I am allowed to do anything.' Yes, but not everything is good for you, I could say that I am allowed to do anything, but I am not going to let anything make me its slave." (Good News Translation Version, I Corinthians. 6.12)

God Knows My Name

My maiden name is, Sharon Cynthia Sinuel. They told me that my mother wanted to name me Sharon and my father wanted to name me Cynthia. So, my mother won out, and Sharon became my first name and Cynthia my middle. From kindergarten on I learned to write my entire name and when I married; I became Sharon Cynthia Calhoun. Sharon Cynthia was the name on my first driver's license, my children's birth certificates, and my bachelor's and masters' degrees.

When I moved to California, I went to the Department of Motor Vehicles, to get a drivers' license. When I presented my Michigan Drivers' License and my birth certificate, they informed me that I couldn't use my middle name, Cynthia, because it wasn't on my birth certificate. It shocked me; all these years I never noticed my middle name wasn't on my birth certificate.

I showed the representative my social security card, a marriage license, and other forms of identification, noting my middle name. The representative explained that because of the new laws concerning an Enhanced Drivers' License, she couldn't put my middle name on my license. I received a California Drivers' License with only my first and last name. Therefore, my new banking accounts, credit cards, and so on; had to match my drivers' license.

It hurt me to lose my middle name; I felt a part of me was gone. I resented that I couldn't use the name given by my parents. I remembered how my father would call me by my middle name. Both of my parents are deceased and all of my younger siblings. To lose my middle name, was akin to losing another part of me.

As I shed a few tears over this loss; I received a message from the Comforter. The Holy Spirit reminded me; God knows my name. God knows me as Sharon Cynthia. I took a deep breath and researched how I could change my name. I often said I would drop my last name of Calhoun because I was divorced, but I kept putting it off. But I will follow up on changing my legal name to the one given me at birth; Sharon Cynthia Sinuel.

Truly Said: Our name is an integral part of our identity.

Scripture: "And the Lord said to Moses, 'I will do the very thing you have asked because I am pleased with you and I know you by name." (New International Version, Exodus. 33.17)

Feel the Heat, or See the Light?

At this specific moment of my career, I was working with clients, who were mandated for treatment. I knew most of the major reasons they were in treatment; court, parents, spouses, and employers. But none of them entered Substance Abuse Treatment voluntarily.

As I had sessions with the clients, my heart was filled with compassion. I listened to all their hurts and losses, from their illegal drug use. It relieved some clients to be mandated for treatment; they weren't ready to volunteer for treatment. These precious people had to go through horrific circumstances because of the consequences of their behaviors. They were in treatment because of "feeling the heat," not because of "seeing the light."

When I finished the last session for the day, I reflected upon my life challenges. I recalled how many times it took the probability of a negative consequence, for me to change. For example, I didn't think of losing weight, until my clothes are too tight, or I didn't reconcile my checkbook until I overdraw it; I had too many examples I could think upon.

As a therapist, I get the benefit of learning from my clients. I knew I needed to change my beliefs concerning change. I didn't want the "heat" of my behaviors, to continually force me to change. I wanted to see the "light." So, I prayed that the Holy Spirit would help me change because I understood the benefits of change. I wanted to change before the "heat" of my negative consequences, forced me to change.

Truly Said: What is going to motivate you to change; the heat or the light?

Scripture: "For you are all children of light, children of the day. We are not of the night or of the darkness." (English Standard Version, I Thessalonians. 5.5)

Who Is the Decision Maker?

I spent the early morning going back and forth with a Customer Service Representative. Because of several exchanges of an item, because of dissatisfaction, I requested a refund. The representative of the company policy informed me; they issue no refunds after 30 days. Despite the policy, I felt I was entitled to a refund and asked to speak with her supervisor. I must have spoken to three more supervisors, up the corporate chain, until I got satisfaction. They gave me a refund.

Later I talked with my sister, over the phone, about this experience. My sister gave me this advice, "Whenever you speak to a customer service representative, before discussing your problem or issue, ask if they are a decision maker? If the representative can't make any exceptions to company policy, you're wasting your time speaking with them."

After we ended our call, I contemplated my sister's suggestion, "Ask if they're a decision maker?"

I pondered upon the spiritual significance of these words. I recalled the circumstances when I was told, "No."

I recalled how many times, Satan taunted me about my prayers being answered and I thought about the times when things appeared utterly hopeless. But the Holy Spirit reminded me that my God intervened and changed all these decisions to my favor. And, I didn't have to go through channel after channel to get to Him!

I thought how blessed I was to know the major decision maker of my life; the Lord my God. And, how blessed I was to know that my God will always have the final say; Amen.

Truly Said: Our God is the court of last resort.

Scripture: "Jesus has the last word on everything and everyone, from angels to armies. He's standing right alongside God, and what he says goes." (The Message Version, Peter .3.22)

Angels All Around

I was a Chemical Dependency Therapist at a maximum-security prison for male inmates. Guards directed the group of inmates to the educational building where I would hold a therapy group. I had to travel across the prison's open yard to get to the building. When I first started, a prison guard would escort me across the yard. Then, I was asked if I felt comfortable walking across the yard by myself; sometimes a guard may not be available. I felt comfortable walking by myself and because it required me to carry a P.P.D. device (personal protective device) at all times. The P.P.D. resembles a pager with a cord, and should I be in danger, I would pull the cord and guards would immediately come to assist me.

As I walked across the yard, I would see inmates on the other side of the yard, and they would call out a greeting or wave. Some inmates were in my group and others I didn't know. This day, one inmate sat in the room, by himself, waiting for the class to start.

When I came in, he said, "I see you're walking across the yard by yourself, now."

I gave no thought to what he said and said, "Yes."

Then he said, "You have nothing to fear walking by yourself because everybody now knows who you are. I'm sure you saw the inmates standing on the other side of the yard; they're watching out for you."

I turned and quickly left the room; I was about to burst into tears. I went to the restroom, stood at the sink, and cried. I was so humbled and touched. These inmates, these men were in prison for criminal offenses; respected and appreciated me. Obviously, my group of inmates informed the others, who I was, and were told to look out for me.

I got myself together and taught the class. We always had a good time in the group, as we all learned, shared, and joked together.

When I got in my car, to drive home, my heart was still tender. I felt honored by what the inmate told me. As I drove, I had an epiphany. I didn't know there were inmates watching me; they were my angels. And, I thanked God, for his angels that surrounded me daily; unseen but protecting me.

Truly Said: Angels are God's secret agents; unseen but battle-ready!

Scripture: "For it is written, 'He will command his angels concerning you, to guard you." (English Standard Version, Luke .4.10)

Fruit of the Womb

My grandmother used to tell me this, concerning my children, "When they're little they're on your feet, when they're older they're on your heart."

Oh, how true this is! Years ago, I was thinking about my children, who were young adults. No longer could I punish their bad behaviors by grounding them or taking away their allowance. I had to accept that they were adults, and I couldn't make them do anything. But I worried about them. Sometimes, their actions made me wonder, *Are they saved?*

Yet, I knew it saved them, but some of their choices could bring about adverse consequences.

This day, I was praying for my three sons, and I was just discouraged because I hadn't seen the manifestation of my prayers.

Then, the Holy Spirit brought to mind, this scripture, "Behold, children are a heritage from the Lord, the fruit of the womb a reward." (Psalm 127:3)

Then the Holy Spirit placed this question in my thoughts, *Do you believe my words?*

I thought, *Yes.*

Then another question, *So, you believe the fruit of the womb is your reward?*

I thought, again, *Yes.*

Then the Holy Spirit asked me a question that blew me away, "You believe your sons, the fruit of the womb, are your reward. So, do you think I would give you a reward that didn't glorify me?"

I sat stunned at these words. I received an assurance that it didn't matter what I see as negative in my sons. Over time, my sons will become men of God and glorify him in their Christian walk. Hallelujah!!

Truly Said: My children will live as my reward!

Scripture: "Train up a child in the way he should go, and when he is old, he will not depart from it." (New King James Version, Proverbs .22.6)

It's a Process

I can't count the many times, when I have told someone I'm a counselor/therapist, and they responded with, "Anybody can do that."

Then some will continue to remark, "It really doesn't take a lot of time to just tell people what to do."

I've had to admit that these statements really irk me. But I didn't know how to respond. I didn't want to offend anyone, yet I didn't know how to present a simple understanding of counseling/ therapy.

Certainly, interventions with a client can be directive. I will give suggestions, guide them to other services, show positive behaviors, and other instructions. However, the major intervention in the therapy process is to deal with/overcome resistance.

Most clients know they have a problem, can identify a problem behavior, or have an idea of how to overcome an issue. No one has to tell most addicts that their drug use is problematic. So, if a client knows they have a problem and knows how to overcome that problem, why aren't they doing it? Simply put; resistance.

When I'm with a client, I also assess, are they unwilling or unable to deal with their issue; or is it a combination of both? Sometimes, for whatever reason, a client's resistance stems from an inability to change; perhaps they don't know how. And sometimes, a client's resistance stems from an unwillingness to change; they're afraid.

I've thought about the reason people may believe counseling someone is easy and directive. Then, I had an "a-ha" moment. Today in our world, we have become accustomed to the idea of things to be quick and fast. The thought can be that counseling is an easy or swift process. And that is just not the case.

After that moment of clarity, I received the words to respond to people, who may not understand therapy. My response will be that therapy is about change. And change is what happens over time; there isn't anything quick about the process.

Truly Said: Therapy is not a microwave process.

Scripture: "There is a time for everything and a season for every activity under the heavens." (New International Version, Ecclesiastes. 3.1)

Advice to a Young Woman

I saw on the news, how a young woman's date, got involved in an altercation with another man. The other man-made some offensive comments concerning the young woman's body. I saw the picture of the young woman's attire, and it exposed much of the generous top portion of her body. I also have seen on the news, when a young woman's malevolent remarks to a man, put her companion in a position of defending her.

Now, I don't want to be an "old fogie." I don't want to be a senior woman, who constantly makes critical remarks about the dress or behaviors of this younger generation of women. I know a judgmental attitude towards the younger generation; will hinder my witness and ability to win them to Christ.

After watching the scenario, I had a revelation. I thought about how actresses, and famous people, have bodyguards when they are out in public. These bodyguards have extensive training on how to protect their employers and themselves. The dates or companions of actresses/actors/famous people aren't expected to or have the responsibility to protect them. So, this was my given revelation; why would a young woman put her date in the position of being a bodyguard?

From my revelation, I will share this advice with a young woman. I will ask the young woman to think about what they will wear, how they will conduct themselves, and what they will say when they go out in public on a date. I would advise them to carry themselves and dress in such a manner that they will not put their date/companion into the role of your bodyguard.

Truly Said: Your date should be your companion, not your bodyguard!

Scripture: "Therefore let us not pass judgment on one another any longer, but rather decide never to put a stumbling block or hindrance in the way of a brother." (English Standard Version, Romans. 14.3)

Jesus Bought My Ticket

I had a dream that I was at a train station. I saw the train coming, and I was so excited. I knew I would ride on that train and going on a journey. I looked behind me and saw a man buying two tickets. I recognized the man to be my Lord and Savior; Jesus Christ. It assured me that I would go on a journey, and Jesus would join me.

I awoke from the dream and I knew it had some meaning on the decisions I needed to make. I had to decide, when I retired, to move to California or stay in my home state of Michigan.

As I sat quietly, I had several revelations that brought me peace. First, Jesus was buying my ticket. Second, Jesus knew where I was going. And third, and most important of all, Jesus would go with me.

The dream provided the answer; I would be on a journey to California. I've written before, that I rarely remember my dreams. But the Holy Spirit knew, how much I needed to receive direction, and he knew what method to use.

Truly Said: We cannot put God in a box; he will get the answers to us, by any means necessary.

Scripture: "The heart of man plans his way, but the Lord establishes his steps." (Psalm. 16.9)

Let It Come to You!

My son and I were watching television.

Playfully, he tossed a small ball and said, "Catch it, Ma."

I tried to catch it, but I dropped it, and we both laughed. He tossed it several times and again, I dropped it.

He laughed, and then instructed me, "Ma, don't grab at the ball, let it come to you."

I took his advice, and I caught the ball. We laughed and I asked him to toss it to me, for a second time. I caught the ball again, and we spent a few minutes, playing catch in my living room.

That night, I thought about what he said, *Don't grab the ball, let it come to you.*

As I pondered, I received a spiritual instruction, "Don't grab for it, let it come to you."

I remembered the times, I tried to grab for something in life, and it didn't happen. Then, I had another thought, *Grabbing at the ball, is akin to trying to get something before its time.* I had been trying to catch the ball prematurely. And I could specifically relate these words to trying to make the vision for my life a reality.

The older I get, the more I realize; timing is about everything. Just because something doesn't happen when I want; doesn't mean all is lost.

Truly Said: You don't have to grab your vision; God will let it come directly to you.

Scripture: "For still the vision awaits its appointed time; it hastens to the end—it will not lie. If it seems slow, wait for it: it will surely come, it will not delay." (Habakkuk .2.3)

He Knows the Future

I had been divorced, with three children. In raising them, I experienced the usual challenges of a single parent; lack of finances, child-care problems, raising sons without a father, and more. I remarried and then; we found out I was pregnant. It thrilled my current husband and me. I was so ecstatic to have a child that would be raised with two parents, in a Christian home. I prepared everything in our lives to receive a child.

However, I had a tubal pregnancy and lost the child. It devastated me. I was looking forward to having a baby where I didn't need to be concerned with finances, child-care, transportation raising a child on my own. I wouldn't have to deal with the quarrels between myself and the ex-husband, concerning our differences on how to raise our sons. I had to grieve and accept the loss of the dream I had for this child.

Fast forward 12 years. My husband committed adultery. I was determined to repair and save the marriage. But it takes two to save a marriage, and the husband wasn't ready to put in the effort. So, I got a divorce.

I was blindsided by this reality and panicked. *Would I be able to live on only my salary?* We had to sell the house;

where would I live? I became so lethargic. I knew I was depressed, yet I had to get myself together. I took time off work and saw a therapist.

During this time, I reflected upon my life and my future. Then, I wondered, what if my child had been born and was now 12 years old? I would have to figure out how to care for the child, deal with her father, look for a place, get enough child-support, and work to stabilize my emotions. I became overwhelmed by thinking about this, *What if? I had a difficult time, simply working to manage my life?*

I took a deep breath, to stop my ruminations, and then I had a catharsis. I received a depth of healing, for the child I lost. God knew this divorce would happen. He knew the challenges I would have, if I had to be a single parent, for the second time. He knew the emotional toll it would take on the child. I had to believe that God knew would be best for me and the child.

Despite all the confusion in my life, I still grieve for this child. I don't want to say, God took the baby away from me. I just want to say God knew the future.

Truly Said: Nothing is hidden from God.

Scripture: "For I know the plans I have for you, declares the Lord, plans for welfare and not for evil, to give you a future and a hope." (Jeremiah. 29:11)

Shifting into the Next Gear

I was chatting with my son concerning how to identify that our prayers are being heard. We shared scriptures that provide the assurance that God heard our petitions. We also shared several scriptures written of reasons our prayers are not heard (and I paraphrase); if we have sin in our heart, God will not hear us, we are praying amiss, and we aren't praying according to His will. We also shared the scripture that states; God always hears our prayers. We continued to discuss how our faith provides us the confidence our prayers are being heard on high.

Then, I shared with him a personal revelation, of my experiences with prayer. Years ago, I was praying quietly. Suddenly, the tone of my voice changed; it was as if I was resolute or defiant. I sensed that I was commanding in my prayers. Now, this experience was far away from my normal voice and posture. I had a consciousness of a Holy Presence surrounding me. My words evoked emotions building up to a crescendo. Subsequently, my emotions appeared to ebb, my voice was lower, and I was back to myself!

I told my son that I sat back and wondered, *What took place?* I had this discovery; my prayer was comparable to driving a stick shift. My prayer began in first gear and accelerated until it went into second gear. I was convinced of my prayers being in complete alignment with the will of heaven and there was a shift in the spirit. However, sometimes I didn't remember what was the essence of my petitions?

I discussed, further with my son, this experience. The next day I began to pray and was ready for another similar encounter; it didn't happen. I wondered, *Why?* But I recognized that this spiritual encounter, wouldn't be a common one; because it had nothing to do with me! This encounter was divinely orchestrated from on High. I didn't have scripture about it and wouldn't use scripture out of context to explain it.

My son and I finished the conversation, with this understanding; prayer and our time with God is personal. And the Holy Spirit will use all of our senses and awareness of our personality to impart confidence in our prayers.

Truly Said: "Our prayers and time with the Holy Spirit is intimate and should not be compared to another's encounter."

(Please note. I chose not to find a scripture to simply fit this devotion; it is a personal encounter that can't be explained specifically by a biblical text!)

I'll Keep Out of His Way!

My son had an outstanding moving violation ticket. I continued to remind him to pay it. I warned if he should get picked up; I wouldn't bail him out. Sure enough, he called his brother; he was in jail and needed his bond to be paid. I wrestled whether I should let him stay in jail overnight and let it be a lesson learned, or to bond him out. The mother in me won out, and I prepared to go out to him. Then I heard a thought, *Why do you feel that you're the only one who can help get him out?*

I sat down and tried to process the thought. Perhaps, I surmised, my son had called another family member to get him out. I kept quiet, to see if the Holy Spirit had any other information for me. I looked up and saw my son at my bedroom door. It shocked me. I asked, "How did you get out?"

My son told me the circumstances that led to his release. He got the ticket in the city but was picked up by the police from a small suburb. The police officer took him to the station and let him make a phone call before putting him in a cell. Shortly, the police officer came and let him go. My son was told that the officer who processed warrants, was sick with the flu and had to go home. In addition, the police officer that manned the front desk was also sick and was on their way home. They were closing down because there wouldn't be anyone to run the station. The officer let my son go and was told to go to the city and pay the ticket. The providence of God was at work. My son was so geeked because he knew it was God, who intervened on his behalf.

I was speechless. After my son left my bedroom, I sat on the bed and had an "a-ha" moment. The Holy Spirit was telling me to stop trying to be my children's savior. I had to stop hindering their faith and reliance on God, by thinking I was the only one to rescue them. I had to learn to keep out of God's way.

Truly Said: God wants to build faith in our loved ones; we need to keep out of His way!

Scripture: "When the righteous cry for help, the Lord hears and delivers them out of all their troubles." (Psalm.34.17)

No Substitutions!

I was at lunch with a group of co-workers. The waiter came to our table to take our orders. The first person to order asked if they had a clear soda and what was the brand? The waiter told her of the brand, and she wrinkled her nose in distaste. She reluctantly said that she would try the brand. Then she made her entrée choice but requested the meat be broiled and not fried. She omitted and asked to substitute several items on her order. For example, she asked to omit the onions, tomatoes, substitute the vegetable, and so on. The rest of us rolled our eyes and sighed to each other. She was wasting our lunchtime.

Finally, all the orders were given to the waiter. When the waiter brought our drinks, she tasted the clear soda; but was dissatisfied and complained that they didn't have the brand she wanted. We finished our lunch and rushed back; we were running late. I went back to my office and thought of the behaviors of my co-worker, with redoing the restaurants' menu to suit her taste. I began to chuck and then I had an epiphany; my co-worker's behaviors mimicked some of our behaviors towards salvation and the gospel.

There are times, I have wondered about the Lord's Commandments and wondered wanted to make substitutions. How about loving our neighbor, only if your neighbor loves you back? I had a further epiphany, when we make a commitment to join a club or an organization, we look loo over the rules and accept them as a requirement for our membership. *Why do we think we can join this "Christianity Club" and redo the rules to our satisfaction?*

I pondered over these thoughts and applied them to my life and walk with Christ. I had to accept that God's "rules" are not made to control us. We can't make any substitutions, for the gospel of Jesus Christ; the gospel is for our safety and our good!

Truly Said: The Gospel menu isn't a la carte.

Scripture: "Everything that I command you, you shall be careful to do. You shall not add to it or take from it." (Deuteronomy. 12.32)

Adult to Adult

My mother and I had a conflictual relationship. She spoke her mind, and we used to call her "sister no mercy." As a child, if I displeased her, she would stop talking to me and this behavior continued into my adulthood. She would be emotionally abusive with her words.

But she had mental health problems, which I wasn't aware of as a child. When I became a therapist, I understood that it depressed her; and her depression fueled her anger. My mother also had panic attacks and was prone to "night terrors" and many a night, as a child we would wake up to her screaming in her sleep.

As a child, my mother had a thyroid disease and had her thyroid removed. I knew not much about her condition in 1930, and she had to spend a year in the hospital. After being discharged from the hospital, they sent her to a girls' school to complete high school. At the school, she learned to be, what I would call today, a nursery school assistant or childcare worker.

My mother was a babysitter for her grandchildren and other people. It was strange to us, that she would be so nurturing to toddlers, but as the children became older; she would withdraw emotionally from them.

I was a shy and very emotional child, and my mother wasn't nurturing, and her cruel words caused me to withdraw from her. As an adult, our relationship became conflictual because I would stand up to her abusive words and weeks would pass, before we would speak.

This particular day, I was praying to be more forgiving towards my mother. I had a catharsis from the words that came to mind. The words instructed me to see my mother from the eyes of an adult. I had been seeing my mind from the eyes of a hurt child, who couldn't understand the experiences that shaped my mother's behaviors.

I was told to remember how my mother clothed and fed us, despite my father's drinking and gambling away the family's finances. I was told to recall hearing her cry when my father would come home with empty pockets. I was reminded that she was a single parent who had an absentee husband. I remember how her sisters would tell of her personality as a young woman: she was a timid and gentle soul. I had an epiphany; my mother was forced in many ways, to harden her emotions, to provide for her children.

I cried, during this time of revelations. I could s see similar traits in us. I understood the emotional and physical challenges of raising children as a single parent. I stopped viewing my mother from the eyes of a child. I was now her adult child and would see her through different eyes; woman to woman. I could emphasize our common struggles.

Truly Said: To grow in our parental relationships, we must see on another through adult eyes.

Scripture: "When I was a child, I spoke as a child, I understood as a child, I thought as a child; but when I became a man, I put away childish things.” (New King James Version, 1 Corinthians .13.11)

He's Got Your Number!

My mother had many aphorisms or sayings. I can remember her saying to me, "I've got your number." This is what she meant, "I know all about you; I know all your behaviors."

I was in therapy with a man, who was a Christian. He was in danger of losing his job because of his drinking. Whenever he had an argument with his wife, he would become angry, and get so drunk that he couldn't go to work. We discussed alternative strategies to manage his emotions. However, after several sessions, he dropped out of therapy. After a few months, he called; he had lost his job and wanted to resume his counseling sessions.

When the call ended, I had this epiphany; Satan had his number. Satan knew all about him; his behaviors and how he would respond in specific situations. Satan knew what number to dial! I knew this "truth" wasn't simply about the client; it was about me. In my life, Satan knew what number to dial.

The bible says, "Satan goes about seeking whom to devour." This means Satan is always watching us. He knows our "hot buttons"; what will set us off. I had to identify my hot buttons, examine my responses, and behaviors. When my behaviors, actions, and responses, align with the word of God, I can disconnect Satan's call and block my number.

Truly Said: "Refuse to allow Satan to get your number."

Scripture: "So that we may not be taken advantage of by Satan. For we are not ignorant of his schemes." (2 Corinthians. 2.11)

Win Win

I disagreed with one of my staff members. I wanted to move towards a solution to the conflict, by identifying where we both could agree. However, this person wanted to resolve the conflict, by getting me to agree that they were "right." I certainly could see their point of view, but I felt they should be open to look at my point of view. I became frustrated as they pressed me to accept their view of the situation.

Finally, I said, "Let's stop and we will revisit this issue, at another time."

The person left in a huff.

I felt discouraged as I walked to my office. I truly wanted to clear up the issue. Then I had a thought, *My staff wanted to win.* My staff member wanted to debate; in a debate, somebody wins!

As a therapist, I learned the reason most people retreat from conflict. They retreat from conflict because of this erroneous belief; somebody has to "win" and somebody has to "lose." Yet, the practical result of a conflict is to identify common ground, or to make compromises, to have a "win-win" conclusion.

I wanted both of us to get some of what we needed. So, I thought over the disagreement. I examined ideas, where we could resolve the issue, by identifying where we could have a "win-win." I wanted both of us to get some of what we wanted.

Truly Said: In a debate, someone wins, and someone loses. Conflicts aren't debates; both can win.

Scripture: "So then, we must always aim at those things that bring peace and that help strengthen one another."

(Good News Version, Romans.14.19)

That Ended It!

One time, as I petitioned God in my prayers, and I had this thought, *Why don't I believe that God will answer, "Yes?"* I had to stop my prayers and consider this thought. I knew if I ask God according to His will and His promises, I will receive what I asked. *So, why would I have to be reminded that God will say, "Yes?"*

Thus, I thought, *While I'm praying, I am certain that God will give me what I asked.* But while waiting for the manifestation of my petitions, I questioned if God would say, "Yes."

So, I thought, *What leads me to doubt?*

I doubted when God says "yes" because it doesn't happen in my time frame. I doubted when God says "yes" when I have already figured out, how God will manifest His answer. I doubted God's "yes" by doing things naturally to help Him along. And most of all, I doubted God saying "yes" because I continued to ruminate and question with "what if?"

As a child, my father would say after he punished us, or chastised us, "That ended it." My father meant this; there wasn't more to say, he wouldn't say anything more about it, and that it was finished end of story!

Thinking about my father; I had an epiphany. Just like my earthly father, my heavenly father, wanted me to have this assurance. My God has said, "Yes." There's no more to think about or do; *that ended it!*

Truly Said: "God said it; end of story."

Scripture: "For all the promises of God in Him are Yes, and in Him Amen, to the glory of God." (New King James Version, 2 Corinthians.1.20)

Take Up Your Cross Daily

As Christians we're familiar with hearing, "Take up your cross daily." I prepare to start my daily devotions, by listening to five-minute teaching. This day, the pastor gave a great explanation of what this means. To take up your cross daily means; be ready to and willing to interrupt your day.

I meditated upon this explanation and received a personal revelation; I hate to have my day, or my plans interrupted. I have a tendency to procrastinate and therefore, I discipline my life by planning my day. Also, I try not to overextend myself or become overly tired. And, I have some symptoms of Attention Deficit Disorder and I have to work on being focused. Because, I know my limitations, I try to order my day and become frustrated if I have to make the slightest adjustment.

So, what does interrupting my day, have to do with taking up my cross daily? For me, it means if I get an unction to pray, I stop what I'm doing and pray. It means if someone needs my help, I change my plans for the day and help. It means if someone calls and needs a listening ear, I don't count the minutes that I'm on the call. And it also means, when I'm reading my friends' Facebook statuses and they ask for prayer; I stop and pray right then and there!

Certainly, I can identify many other examples, of interrupting my day to take up my cross daily. Now, this is how I must start my day. I must ask the asking the Holy Spirit to give me the grace, patient, and willingness, to when I have His unction; to stop and adjust my day!

Truly Said: "Stop, look, and listen!"

Scripture: "The heart of a man plans his way, but the Lord establishes his steps." (English Standard Version, Proverbs.16.9)

Copyright Notes

---

[i] New Life Version, copyright © 1969 and 2003. Used by permission of Barbour Publishing, Inc., Uhrichsville, Ohio 44683. All rights reserved

[ii] All Scripture quotations are taken from THE MESSAGE, copyright © 1993, 2002, 2018 by Eugene H. Peterson. Used by permission of NavPress. All rights reserved. Represented by Tyndale House Publishers, Inc

[iii] Scripture quotations marked (NIV) are taken from the Holy Bible, New International Version®, NIV®. Copyright © 1973, 1978, 1984, 2011 by Biblica, Inc.™ Used by permission of Zondervan. All rights reserved worldwide.

[iv] The ESV® Bible (The Holy Bible, English Standard Version®), copyright © 2001 by Crossway, a publishing ministry of Good News Publishers. Used by permission. All rights reserved

[v] Scripture quotations marked (CEV) are from the Contemporary English Version Copyright © 1991, 1992, 1995 by American Bible Society. Used by Permission.

[vi] THE HOLY BIBLE, NEW INTERNATIONAL VERSION®, NIV® Copyright © 1973, 1978, 1984, 2011

by Biblica, Inc.™ Used by permission. All rights reserved worldwide

[vii] Scripture is taken from GOD'S WORD®. © 1995, 2003, 2013, 2014, 2019, 2020 by God's Word to the Nations Mission Society. Used by permission.

[viii] Scripture taken from the New King James Version®. Copyright © 1982 by Thomas Nelson. Used by permission. All rights reserved.

I dedicate *Truly Said Devotionals – Volume One* to the people over the years, who have asked me, how does God speak to people?

Sharon Calhoun is a licensed clinical social worker (Michigan). In her 30 years of professional experience, she has worked in community mental health, outpatient and residential mental health/substance abuse programs and in a maxim security prison, with over 30 years' experience as a therapist.

She has retired from her last position as a clinical supervisor, with the Salvation Army Residential Substance Abuse Program. After retirement she moved to California; however, she travels back and forth to her home state of Michigan. Currently, she works part-time as a therapist in an online platform.

Sharon has worshipped and lived as a Christian for 33 years.